Death of England: Closing Time

Clint Dyer and Roy Williams

T0179859

methuen | drama

LONDON • NEW YORK • OXFORD • NEW DELHI • SYDNEY

METHUEN DRAMA
Bloomsbury Publishing Plc
50 Bedford Square, London, WC1B 3DP, UK
1385 Broadway, New York, NY 10018, USA
29 Earlsfort Terrace, Dublin 2, Ireland

BLOOMSBURY, METHUEN DRAMA and the Methuen
Drama logo are trademarks of Bloomsbury Publishing Plc

First published in Great Britain by Methuen Drama in 2023

A catalogue record for this book is available from the British Library.

A catalog record for this book is available from the Library of Congress.

ISBN: PB: 978-1-3504-4882-7
ePDF: 978-1-3504-4883-4
eBook: 978-1-3504-4884-1

Series: Modern Plays

Typeset by Mark Heslington Ltd, Scarborough, North Yorkshire

To find out more about our authors and books visit
www.bloomsbury.com and sign up for our newsletters.

Death of England: Closing Time

Clint Dyer and Roy Williams

The Company, in alphabetical order:

Denise **Jo Martin**
Carly **Hayley Squires**

Football Commentary **Will Close and Gunnar Cauthery**
Coronation Commentary **John Hodgkinson and Nick Fletcher**

Additional Limo Passengers **Kate Kelly Flood, Lola Shalam, Rebecca Hyde, Mia Austen, Ruba Ahmed, Laura Glover, Emma Wright, Afrya Nylander and Adwoa-Alexsis Mintah**

Director **Clint Dyer**
Co-Set and Costume Designers **Sadeysa Greenaway-Bailey and ULTZ**
Lighting Designer **Jackie Shemesh**
Co-Sound Designers **Benjamin Grant and Pete Malkin**
Dialect Coach **Hazel Holder**
Company Voice Work **Cathleen McCarron**
Associate Director **Mumba Dodwell**

Producer **Adwoa-Alexsis Mintah**
Production Manager **Vivienne Clavering**
Dramaturgs **Sasha Milavic Davies and Ola Animashawun**
Stage Manager **Jo Phipps**
Deputy Stage Manager **Ben Donoghue**
Assistant Stage Manager **Fana Sunley-Smith**
Assistant Stage Manager (Rehearsals) **Helen Stone**
Assistant Set and Costume Designer **Seonaid Gowdie**
Project Draughting **Tom Atkinson, Jef Gage, Janet Williamson, Nathan James**
Digital Art **Daniel Radley-Bennett, Emma Pile, Madeleine Dymond, Ruth Badila, Natalie Johnson, Seonaid Gowdie**
Costume Supervisor **Ysanne Tidd**
Wigs, Hair & Make-up Supervisor **Leah O'Connell**
Running Wardrobe Supervisor **Amanda Tyrrell**
Prop Supervisor **Matilde Marangoni and Kinga Czynciel**
Props Coordinator **Michelle McLucas**
Lighting Supervisor **Sam Mcleod**
Lighting Programmer **Reese Graham**
Rehearsal Lighting Programmer **Chris Shute**

Production Sound Engineer **Sam Digney**
Sound Operator **Ben Vernon**
Stage Supervisor **Lee Harrington**
Rigging Supervisor **Mike Rungen**
Automation **Thomas Russell**
Construction Supervisor **Barrie Nield**
Scenic Art Supervisor **Cass Kirchner**
Production Photographer **Feruza Afewerki**

Opening
Dorfman Theatre, 20 September 2023

For Stephen S. Thompson.

Rest in eternal power.

Death of England: Closing Time

Characters

Denise, *black, early fifties*
Carly, *white, early thirties*

Scene One

Carly *and* **Denise** *stand. They are waiting.* **Denise** *looks to the floor seething. We are outside the shop. Their shop. The family shop.*

Carly *looks to us and nods a hello. She looks to* **Denise** *who still cannot raise her eyes.*

We hear a football match on the radio. The Orient are playing. We can also hear the live sound from the actual stadium.

Denise   I was outraged.

Carly   I was fucking outraged.

Denise   Do you mind?

Carly   Mind?

Denise   It's me one, talking to them.

Carly (*sighs; to the audience*)   And here we go.

Denise   *Here we go?* What a gal, renk!

Carly   What's yer beef, Denise?

Denise   Yu mek joke? Is that a joke?

Carly   Obviously, in general, I am aware of what has been making your piss boil over the last few weeks, I just thought it might have been something else.

Denise   There is no room in my life for anything else, don't you get it?

Carly   I get it, I get it!

Denise (*points to the shop*)   Look at it, Carly, look at my dream.

Carly   Our dream!

We see a 'For Sale' sign.

Denise   Just let me speak for a minute, can you do that?

Carly   Gawn den!

Denise (*to the audience*)   I have never told anyone this except my son, and Miss Dennison when she held me back for detention one time, but it has always been a dream of mine to be a chef. End up working in some fine dine restaurant, running my own kitchen. I would start out by having my own shop first. My very own West Indian cafe. Beef patties on sale there, right in front, with your rice and peas, your curried goat, ackee and saltfish, the usual suspects. Made fresh, every day. By me! And quality service, mi tell you. I told Delroy, straight off, when he come to me with this, I told him, I told my boy:

'You're gunna have to put a shift in, we will have to graft, like 24/7.'

I said masking my total glee with the tone of a party political broadcast . . . which was weird cos I fuckin' hate 'em.

'If I get so much as a smell of the chat fast, work slow ting, which too many black people have become accustomed to, yes I said it, deh done!'

Delroy   'Yeah but we don't have to /'

Denise   'Deh gone, deh out! Do not pass go, do not collect 200 pounds!'

Delroy   'Aright /'

Denise   To see as well as hear my boy beg. Then he bit his lip in that way he's done since he was three . . . and his liquid eyes glistened at me with hope.

Delroy   'Just imagine it! Carly and Michael selling their flowers one end, you and me on the other, selling your hot patties! One day I can take over completely, then you can go off and be a chef like you always wanted. It'll work, Mum.'

He sold it to me, in spite of my reservations, of which there were plenty. Namely, us. Going into business, with them! The Fletchers! Shops and restaurants closing left and right,

post-pandemic. And don't even get me started on my energy
bills.

(*Gestures to an audience member.*) Yeah, you dun know. A whole
firm of them claarts, multi-billionaires, teifin' us all blind!
And yet in spite of all that, me and my stupid arse self signs
on the dotted line for them lot. Lawd Jesus, what was I
thinking?

Carly   Have you finished then?

Denise   Girl, I barely started.

Carly   I know /

Denise   Oh look she knows . . . You do? Do you?

Carly   Damn sure I do.

Denise   I know you fink ya do but . . . it's different /

Carly   Different?

Denise   For you, yeah.

Carly   Coz I'm white?

Denise   Cos you're young! . . . You're young and you're
stupid.

Carly   De /

Denise   And I'm old! I'm old and stupid. I am so bloody
stupid.

Carly   No /

Denise   I should never have trusted those two.

Carly   It wasn't /

Denise   Really . . . are you gonna really /

Carly   No . . . I'm not gonna but /

Denise   But what? . . . What fucking exactly did you not
hear?

Carly   I heard.

Denise   Obviously, not hard enough.

Carly   Go on. Get it off your chest, Denise. Finish up.

Denise   That was my savings, thirty years of savings, thirty
years of yes sirs, no sirs, of course sirs, I must have got it
wrong sirs, eating shit from people not fit to wipe my arse let
alone my shoes . . . certainly not fit to be a boss over me.
Men . . . men with an IQ the size of their dick in inches. Men
with eyes glazing at the idea of parity . . . flinching at the
notion they may have to stop pinching a woman's arse for
sport . . . even though I run the bloody ward . . . Literally
not knowing how to talk to you if they can't flirt with you . . .
not knowing how to praise you without making you feel
small . . . Men! With no idea I'm sweating not because I'm in
need of HRT but because I'm trying so hard not to hang 'em
from their crass coloured, I'm so characterful, but educated,
right on, waffle tie. When you've worked that long . . . for
men . . . entitled, alcoholic men for thirty years . . . and
saved the only thing that can make it worth it . . . money!
And then lose it because . . . because of a man you gave
'birth' to . . . then come back to me . . . and tell me it's not
different.

Carly   Hold up, stop!

Denise   Say what?

Carly   Jus rewind and pull up a sec.

Denise   Don't do that that, Carly. Not today.

Carly   Eh?

Denise   That.

Carly   What?

Denise   That! What you just did . . . patois, bad bloody
patois at that . . . just . . . don't . . . Not today.

Carly   Aawydi raa /

Denise   I said /

Carly   That ain't /

Denise   Yes it is! Everything I have, everything I have built is about to be taken away by the man who is coming for these.

(*Holds up a set of keys.*) So, not today, girl, you hear?

Carly   Shall we just wait for him to come in silence then?

Denise   Wise words.

Carly   Fine . . . mind if I listen to the footie.

Denise   Not at all.

Carly *puts on the radio from her phone.*

Orient and Manchester United are still playing in a League Cup match.

Denise   Well, at least they're enjoying themselves.

Carly   Michael and Delroy?

Denise   No, Carly, Ant and fucking Dec. Who do you think?

Carly   Wise words?

Denise   Oh yeah . . . yeah . . . silence.

Carly   Yeah. Silence is very good.

Denise   Why don't you try it then?

Carly   It's good, cos you don't wanna get me . . .

Denise   Mad?

Carly   Started, Denise. Started. It was my shop as well. My mum's shop. My dad's shop.

Denise   Your point.

Carly   The point I am trying to make is that I've got grievances too, you know.

Denise   I'll bet . . . you live with the fool that I have the misfortune to call a son, and you're the sister of the other fool . . . grievances . . . you should 'ave a rahtid vendetta.

Carly   Shall we?

Denise   Yes. Yes. silence.

They listen to the game and the Orient nearly score. They can't help but react.

Denise   Can you imagine their faces?

Carly   Michael must be having a seizure by now.

Denise   Delroy, too.

Carly   So, about the silence?

Denise   Oh, shut up. You know what?

Carly   What?

Denise   They should be here. They should be doing this. Waiting for the man.

Carly   What difference does it make who is here?

Denise   We all had a stake in this, it is symbolic.

Carly   Bollocks more like.

Denise   They should be here, Carly.

Carly   Leyton Orient at home, playing against Man U in a League Cup match! You expect them to miss that? Come alive, Denise. That would have been . . . I mean, like, dat would have mash dem up for real.

Denise   Yes . . . I guess that would have been the last straw . . . Poor lickle youths gunna miss a game of footie. I had plans today. How much by the hour are you paying that babysitter?

Carly   No one's 'appy, Denise . . .

Denise   Dat's right is it? . . . (*To audience.*) Anyone happy? Anyone at all?

(*To* **Carly**.) Looks like you're bloody right and all . . . no one is happy . . . well done you.

Carly   I mean about the shop . . . (*To audience.*) In case you ain't figured it out . . .

Denise   Of course they've figured it out, they look stupid to you?

Carly   We're selling the florist . . . dat's why we are here /

Denise   And takeaway.

Carly   And takeaway /

Denise   The newly bought florist and takeaway.

Carly   It's hardly newly bought /

Denise   In shop years it is . . . imagine it's a cat . . .

Carly   A cat?

Denise   In cat years it's still pooing in ya yukka plant pot . . . it's newly bought.

Carly   We tried! . . . Michael tried, Delroy tried . . . we all tried!

Denise   Not hard enough!

Carly   'kin 'ell! You'd give aspirin a headache.

(*To audience.*) I'm sorry. I'm sorry to . . . shout, but she gets right up my . . . you know like she's not to blame at all.

Denise   How am I to blame?

Carly   You serious?

Denise   Well, yes . . . actually . . . I'm deadly serious.

Carly   You been a stubborn cow for one.

Denise   Excuse me?

Carly   Not getting your jab.

Denise   Oh!

Carly   Not getting any jabs!

Denise   I might have known you'd bring that up.

Carly (*to the audience*)   I was telling her. I was telling her from time.

Denise   Screeching more like!

Carly   Yer gunna gets Covid! And guess, wat she gets Covid! She lock up her arse fer twenty-one backside days, straight!

Denise   What did I tell you about going all patwa?

Carly   What did I say about not getting a jab?

Denise   I don't trust those jabs /

Carly   But I have to?

Denise   My right! You don't know what's in them.

Carly   Do you know what's inside all these fags you smoke? Aside from murdering freaking nicotine? You know what's done to beef that's inside those patties of yours?

Denise (*outraged*)   Facety bitch!

Carly   Do yer?

Denise   Grass- fed organic beef if you must.

Carly   You know what's sprinkled on the skunk weed you smoke?

Denise   High grade, actually.

Carly   Whatever.

Denise   It wasn't made for black people's DNA /

Carly   Come off it . . . look I'm not saying pharma ain't cunts /

Denise   You dun know you can't /

Carly   But when you're in business with someone, doing something with someone . . . it's all for one and that ain't it?

Denise   It's my right /

Carly   Then don't come later with all this fucking attitude . . . like.

Denise   Like what?

Carly   So it's alright that I kept everything going, kept working, paying *our mortgage* . . . me and Michael spending what's left of our money to try and keep it all going but not you.

Denise   You saying our closure is my fault now? Facety /

Carly   Twenty-one days, not a single pattie made or sold . . . fucking Dr Sebi.

Denise   Delroy was there. He was in charge.

Carly   Delroy ain't you.

Denise   Damn right!

Carly   He can't cook toast!

Denise   On that we agree on. Wurtless eddyaat.

Carly   Just don't come it, alright.

Denise   Ok. Carly you've scored a great goal with that, but don't push your luck, don't push me. Not unless you want them to know how you put the final nail into the coffin of our shops.

Carly   Alright /

Denise   What the rass you were even thinking, I do not know. I fail!

Carly   Ok, how about we just . . . go silent again . . . let's not, you know, bring dem into our . . . erm, SHIT.

Denise   You just did.

Carly   Shall we not anymore? Cos the two men in question have been known to parade our stuff . . . us . . . around in circles that wouldn't . . . let's just say folk that wouldn't knowingly share the same air as us if they didn't have to.

Denise   Unless it's a football match . . . maybe then or, em . . . at the supermarket . . . food and football, eh, the Englishman common ground . . .

Carly   Neutral territory for the masses /

Denise   Yeah a place where no ideas are shared /

Silence.

Carly   Borrowed or /

Denise   Worked through . . . Perfect . . . you know Delroy cried more at Orient's relegation than he did over his dad dying.

Carly   That's not quite fair.

Denise   Really?

Carly   Not quite true either.

Denise   You was thirteen . . . how the hell would you /

Carly   I'm there now . . . with 'im now /

Denise   What he . . . talks . . . to you about his /

Carly   Yes.

Denise   Delroy?

Carly   Cries in his sleep about his dad.

Denise   Didn't to me . . .

Carly   Oh.

Denise   Right through his teens . . . he didn't.

Carly   Wow.

Denise   Right till now . . . he don't . . . talk to me about him.

Carly   No?

Denise   No?

Carly   Oh . . . well . . .

Silence.

Denise   What does he say?

Carly   Really, you want me to /

Denise   Just /

Carly   But he should tell you himself /

Denise   But he don't . . . won't, will he?

Carly   Then . . . I can't, can I?

Denise   Bet you fucking love dat doh, innit?

Carly   No.

Denise   Look how you nipples a buss tru your blouse . . . turns you right on, innit?

Carly   He'd be upset /

Denise   If you told him . . . maybe if you blabbed, squealed, yeah he'd be put out . . . maybe . . . if he knew . . . so?

Carly   So?

Denise   So don't . . . tell him.

Carly   Denise /

Denise   What did he say? What does he say? What does he . . . how does he talk about his dad?

Silence.

Sound of crowd gasping. **Carly** *and* **Denise** *can hear it through the radio as well.*

Carly   What is the point of spending all of that money on a number 9, when he never plays like a bleeding number 9?

Denise   Why won't you answer my question?

Carly   A couple of minutes ago, according to you he was nothing but a wurtless eddyaat.

Denise   He is still a wurtless eddyaat . . . but he is also my son.

Carly   And my fella!

Denise   How does he talk about his dad?

Carly   Are you sure you want to know?

Denise   Tell me.

Carly   Last time we was in bed . . . while back it was . . . his leg . . . yeah his leg was twitching, that's what woke me . . . which usually means he's dreaming that he's playing footie but when I looked at his face . . . well, his face looked like one dem old staffs, you know . . . even his nose was wrinkled in anguish.

'Babe, you aright? Babe, wake up . . . Delroy, wake up.'

Delroy   'Oh my God . . . God oh . . . oh that was . . . fuck . . . oh fuck, Carly . . . I was, I was . . . my dad, I was strangling my dad . . . I had him by the throat and I . . . I was . . . fourteen . . . me at fourteen but my arms were like a boxer's arms . . .'

Carly   His was face puffy, filled with a whole night of blood, his eyes full to brim with tears.

Delroy   'And my hands . . . were thick man's hands but I'm fourteen and my hands are white, Carly, but it's me, big white hands but they're my hands round his neck and I'm whispering to him, "Don't die . . . don't die, please, please don't die", and I'm killing him, Carly.'

Carly   He pleaded, Dee . . . Unfiltered, unabashed . . . un . . . like him.

Delroy   'And I start to tell him, Carly . . . about my grades and how great I am at maths and how well I'm doing and how it don't mean nothing if he can't see it . . . don't mean shit if he ain't here to smile at me when I get the results . . . All this still with my hands round his neck . . . yeah and I tell him if I don't get his approval, that my efforts are worth it . . . that his fight to raise me is worth it . . . then I ain't worth shit . . . I don't mean shit . . . that if his fight to survive all this racism and bring me up and to stay with Mum for me ain't worth it . . . then 'I' don't mean shit! . . . cos I know most men don't feel good enough about themselves to be themselves, to love themselves enough to stay in a relationship . . . Carly, I went Oprah Winfrey on him . . . while I'm still squeezing his neck /

Carly   I knew there and then . . . in that moment, what he was saying to me should make him mine . . . that he was mine now . . . I felt terrible that I'd made his pain about 'me' but I knew . . . well, thought . . . I'd won him there and then, in his worst moment, I got him . . . he was mine.

'Don't stop /'

I said stroking his stubbled teared-up cheek,

'Let it out /'

Delroy   'Then he stopped breathing . . . no breath just . . . panic in his eyes now . . . as his eyes are getting stiller and stiller, bigger and bigger . . . stiller and stiller . . . but I keep squeezing and my hands start going darker and darker till they're my hands . . . my black hands around his neck and I start to cry, Carly . . . Carly, I cry . . . cry so deep I feel like a breathing through my arse . . . then he's gone and, and, and, and, and . . . something in me is gone . . . a part gone . . . with him . . . a part of me is dead . . . gone . . . That's it . . . it's like there is nothing to prove anymore and don't need to do anything for anyone, I don't owe anyone nothing . . . nothing.'

Denise   Yes, all except my ninety grand.

Carly   You're going to hold onto that, like some Rottweiler, aren't yer!

Denise   He said all that?

Carly   I couldn't make that up.

Denise   What about me?

Carly   I knew I shouldn't have /

Denise   You see dat . . . he tells you that . . . and all I get from him is . . . his love for fucking Orient . . . and white girls . . . wow dat's what he said . . . that's what he says after . . . everything . . . Everything I done . . . did for him . . . /

Carly   It was a dream /

Denise   See dat deh bwoy . . . rah . . . and then I'm here, right here clearing up his mess /

Carly   Our mess . . . it's all our mess

Denise   While he watching the match /

Carly   You said yourself it would be the straw.

Denise   I said he should be here! Yes but . . . what is . . . I mean how can . . . I have done everything for him /

Carly   It was only a dream /

Denise   You see that though? . . . You know . . . that? . . . Like how can a man . . . have all the smarts, ability, strength, yet put all that emotion and love into something that don't love him back . . . I'm here . . . we're here . . . the energy he puts into Orient, the hours, the hope, the /

Carly   They need it /

Denise   You chatting about men? Breaking news here, Carly, all men don't follow football /

Carly   Our men do. Our men love it.

Denise   Yeah more than me /

Carly   No, don't be /

Denise   You put time into the things you love . . . no? You put your heart and passion and dreams and conversation and thinking . . . Into the things you love, and that club, that team, Leyton rhatid Orient, gets more then me . . . his mum, his family . . . it's a business, Carly . . . it's a money-making enterprise . . . locals rarely play for the club now . . . it's not about community . . . and it gets more devotion than we do . . . how?

Carly   He loves you.

Denise   Well, on his planet, love must cost, innit? It must be costing him a fucking ton.

Carly (*pleads*)   Dee!

Denise   You know, he don't ask me how am going to get further up the food chain this year . . . who am I going to get this year to up my chances of winning my goals . . . fulfilling my dream. Doesn't jump for joy when I win a promotion . . . he don't even come a watch me play backgammon at his auntie's club night /

Carly   Well, it's hardly a mic drop of an evening /

Denise   Half the investment he puts into football could feed that homeless hotel on Warwick Street for a year.

Carly   That ain't likely.

Denise   I mean imagine it, Carly . . . if all those fuckers in that stadium put the hours, money and heart they put into football into this country, what a country it would be.

Carly   We pay taxes.

Denise   You know what I'm saying! What if they put all that energy into their women?

Carly   The women who won the Euros?

Denise   Their women! Their daughters! Not a bunch of gal who play far better footie and bring home the trophies only to get paid a tiny fraction of what the man dem get! You know what I am saying, Carly.

Carly   Yes . . . yeah . . . I do /

Denise   This, this shop was my dream and's watching the football and I'm here giving away the keys to some fella I don't even know who's gonna rock up at any moment . . . selling our dream, my dream . . . with you . . . how could he do that . . . after what you did . . . to leave me with you.

Carly   You said all that stuff was unfair /

Denise   It was . . . is . . . don't mean he should have left me with . . . you.

Carly   Let me just do it?

Denise   Shouldn't have to do it on your own.

Carly   I'd leave but nor should you . . . have to . . . do it on your own.

Denise   I guess not.

Carly   Well, lets hope this geezer comes quick then.

Denise   Yeah, Carly, let us hope.

Carly   Who is this bloke anyhow?

Denise   Say?

Carly   This geezer who we are handing the keys to, who is he buying our place for?

Denise   He's not buying for anyone, he's selling it on. Some coffee place, I think.

Carly   Not another bleeding GAIL'S! Please don't tell me.

Denise   Alright, I won't tell you.

Carly   Just what London needs. Another expensive place for privileged middle-class scum to park their arse.

Denise   Dial it down, Carly, I don't business. Yeah?

Carly *looks through one of* **Denise***'s boxes.*

Carly   Oi, oi, so what's all this?

She finds a framed certificate.

Denise   Put that back.

Carly (*reads*)   'It is hereby certified Denise Gloria Tomlin . . .'

Denise   Carly!

Carly (*continues*)   '. . . has passed the level four catering course . . .' Wow, that's à la carte, Denise. When did you . . .

Denise (*snatches the frame from her*)   Enough!

Carly   Oh, what's up with you?

Denise   Not a ting!

Carly   Fucking hell, you're gunna be well alright though, innit? With that you can get a catering job, work in a restaurant. Come on, Denise, it's à la *bleeding* carte!

Denise   You would think.

Carly   Meaning?

Denise   Just leave it, Carly.

The football plays loudly in the background just as there is a near miss on goal.

Carly   Sounds like someone almost scored. Orient, I bet.

Denise   Nope, United.

Carly   How do you know?

Denise   Cos Leyton bloody Orient wouldn't know what a
goal is, never mind actually score one. Don't you know
anything?

Scene Two

Carly (*to the audience*)   Now, before she starts off again, or
before someone actually scores, let's get one thing clear, this
ain't just about the shops, it ain't about the boys living it large
at Orient today, it's about me, it's always been about me.
From when I had my first period, it was about me. Me and
my skin, my nasty white skin taking her sweet little boy away
from her. Mind you, I suppose having a dad like mine didn't
help much.

You probably know by now that my dad, Mister Alan
Fletcher, was a man of his generation, he had tendencies,
and yes many of them were racist. Which wasn't exactly a lot
of fun for me. I suppose a lot of you can see where she is
coming from. But hold up a sec, clear your mind for a
moment. The entire neighbourhood was changing, from the
time Dad was alive.

'Name one corner of London that is exclusively white, and if
it is, it soon won't be. Mark my words.'

He could see London was changing, all of England in fact,
but he still went off on his shit. Rights for whites bollocks. I
will say it again, rights for whites bollocks. Because it is, it is
bollocks, God knows what he would have said about taking
the knee . . . 'They should be grateful' . . . Funny how easy
we forget what the Commonwealth is . . . grateful . . . it's a
mug's game thinking that way, let alone believing. Just so
you know, just so it is clear in your head, as well as
underlined I am not like him, I never was. I might have said
the odd thing, growing up.

Denise   Might of?

Carly   But fair is fair.

Denise   We are here outside because of what you said.

Carly   I know that.

Denise   Your man, the love of your supposedly, is sleeping on the sofa cos of what you said.

Carly   I didn't see any of you in that house where I grew up.

Denise   That's your excuse for what you did /

Carly   Before you pipe up with it, it's important for me they hear this, Denise. You might learn something and all. D'you mind?

Denise   Gwan den.

Carly (*to the audience*)   Growing up, we had no choice in that house, he was still our dad, we had to get along. So, every now and then I had to pretend. That I was all in with him, white must be right. So, you might hear some things for which I am sorry, from the bottom. I repeat, rights for whites bollocks! Now thing is, let's be honest here, Denise and I were never as close as Nadine Dorries's tongue was to Boris Johnson's arse, but if it weren't for her I would never have met him, the love of my life, Delroy! It was like you wake up one day, just any ordinary unremarkable day, but you have got no idea, not a single clue, that you are moments away from having your life changed forever.

It was a day in March, Dad was out here, on the stall, like normal, cutting stems off, giving it large to his customers, old as well as new, as he serves up my favourite bunch, bright purple alliums and white gladioli, three or four daffs, with a touch of red camellia, followed up by some grape hyacinth and magnolia, all nicely tied up with a cord of thick brown twine, in a bow.

Alan   'You want some fruit for that bowl, mate. Don't get aerated.

Just pulling your plonker. What can I do you for?'

Carly   I was his special assistant that day, on account of being suspended from school again. Long story I will not bore you with, except to say Miss Mckenzie my old form teacher was nuttin but a dried-up claart on two legs and she deserved to have that blackboard eraser aimed at her head, and I ain't taking about some old cloth or a tissue. I mean the hard ones, old school. That feels like you've got a brick in your hands.

Anyhow's, Dad's stall.

Alan   'Carly, run to the cafe and get us a cup of PG, skimmed milk, three sugars and a double egg bacon roll with brown sauce. Don't look at me like that.'

Carly   He said that on the account Mum would have a size 10 on the Richter scale meltdown if she found he was off the diet she had put him on.

Alan   'Our little secret, babe.'

Carly   He would say. His rough sausage fingers stroking my face. So there I am, double egg bacon roll in one hand, mug of tea in the other, about to cross the road when I see her, or should I say hear her, Delroy's mum, Miss Sourpuss over . . .

(*Points to* **Denise**.) . . . going well into it with my dad. I couldn't quite make her out from across the road at first, but there she was, her enormous long dreadlocked head against fuchsia, orange and green . . . making her skin glow, then her dreads against the purple and chartreuse-greenish yellow to you, made a Frida Kahlo painting look anaemic. Anyways . . .

I didn't need a crystal ball to work out what was going on, on the account of my droopy big brother with his head down, whilst Denise was flinging a whole heap of lyrics in my dad's face, claiming how racist Michael was to her, calling her a black bitch after she caught him and her son nicking the big school sign and smoking in the park, proper wars they was having, on my dad's stall. He just stood there taking it, giving as good as he got mind . . .

Alan   'My boy ain't like that, if he said what he said we'll be having words . . . your hair looks nice.'

Denise ended it all by telling him to . . .

Denise   Go fuck yourself, as I recall.

Carly   Yeah, you properly dun him! I was well impressed, did I ever tell you that?

(*Back to the audience.*) I was. Dad was shook, I could see it all over, he had never had a black person, let alone a black woman, speak to him like that. You should have clocked his face every time, mostly over dinner, when Michael would be banging on about his new best friend Delroy. Delroy did this, man, Delroy said that, man. Delroy is so funny, Delroy is so sharp. Dad lost it one time by screaming . . .

Alan   'Well, why don't you marry the cunt then?'

Carly   He never did it again, swearing I mean. Mum could take most things, well, she had to, with a family like us, but cursing over the dinner table, nuh, nuh, she weren't having that.

Maggie   'Alan James Fletcher, be told!'

Carly   Dad crossed the line then, he never crossed it again. Michael wasn't helping though. Still going on about his brudda, Delroy. Mum and Dad had well and truly had enough, by now Michael's voice was sounding like fingers on a chalkboard. It was Mum who said the following. She raised her hands in defeat, something she was used to doing, being a Leyton Orient fan, and asked Michael or should I say told . . .

Maggie   'Bring the little gent over, Michael. Let's have a proper look at him then.'

Carly   She said like she was planning to cook him for tea. I was expecting Dad by now to pipe up, come out with something like . . .

Alan   'No you bloody well ain't, not in my house, an Englishman's home is his castle.'

Carly   But no, nothing! He didn't pipe up, not once. He just nodded his head, grunted through his nose and went back to reading *The Sun*.

Maggie   'Wanna meet the offspring of the lady that shut him up.'

Carly   She poked, enjoying Dad's red-faced countenance. I could not believe what I was hearing. Mum wasn't deaf, for years she heard all sorts from Dad, black this, black that. When we were kids, it was her who would send me and Michael to McDonald's with a tenner, and tell us not to come back until Dad and his muggy right-wing mates had left the house.

And now through that same door, she was letting Delroy through. And that was it! From the minute I clapped eyes. It's hard to explain, when you get that feeling, when you see someone you are drawn to for the first time in your natural. I mean, do you know, does anyone know when you clasps eyes on the love of you life straight off, that is the person you are maybe two or three dates away from seeing naked, and they will be seeing you naked. Do you think that, anyone? No mind. I can't recall what it was when I first clapped eyes, I mean he was nice looking and all, I mean most of the black boys around were nice, still are. They gave the chat, they knew how to move themselves around, scrubbed up well, smelt good, knew their music, can't be argued. So, what was it then? What was it about Delroy bloody Tomlin that made me want me to climb him like a tree from the minute he stood in our front door? I remember thinking he had a whiff of Derek about him. You know Derek, from that film back in

the day, *Save the Last Dance*. He was all street but was gunna
be a doctor.

(*To an audience member.*) Yeah, you know! My favourite film
ever, man! I just love it when Derek first meets that white
girl, and they are cussing each other. 'Steps ain't no square
dance. That's alright, I can dance in circles probably around
you.'

Laughs.

Then they get all up close when he teaches her how to dance
like a black person. 'How's my butt doing? It's good girl, it's
nice.' That's how Delroy was, the way he breezed himself in,
but not quite, cos I knew he was putting on a show, cos he
knew about my dad, and he wanted to show him, at least on
the surface, what he was about, even though he was more
likely bricking it. No one saw him come in, no one needs to
see him come out.

But his coolness, the way he clocked me, as I was clocking
him, it was straight out of the ending of that film which
makes me melt all over every time I think about it. You know
when Derek goes, 'You can do it, Sara. Ain't nobody
watching you but me.'

Purrs with delight.

You'd had have it, wouldn't yer? You'd wanna mop him up,
if he came your way! You'd beat down any women to get to
him, admit! Dad couldn't see it. The very idea of his
favourite daughter, his princess, going anywhere near a
'coloured boy' was so offensive to him, it couldn't possibly
happen, he'd believed there was life on Mars before that.
But Mum could. She could see it, she could sense it.

It's the things that mums get but dads don't. When they
realise their precious daughter, their little girl, ain't so little
anymore. She has come of age, she is starting to bloom, is
getting with it, you know, boys noticing yer. Well, it wasn't
happening in the street, it was here right here in his own

home. Mum knew I was pregnant before I did, that is how good she is. What was I supposed to do? Drool myself to death over Delroy and then watch my dad finally put two and two together as soon as Mum has a word in his ear, and lynches him? I had to do something, I had to take action, which is why,

(*Points to* **Denise**.) Before she chimes, I had to say a few things, throw Mum off the scent. I'm not proud, I'm not proud of a lot of other things I may have said.

Denise   You may have said?

Carly   Alright things I did say, but I am guessing we will get to all of that.

The point is back then, I had to act fast as well as think fast to save Delroy's life.

(*To* **Denise**.) Just as I was trying to save his life a few weeks back, both of our lives in fact, trying to save the shops.

Denise   That don't cut it, Carly.

Carly   I was /

Denise   Cha /

Carly   I was . . . just like I was back then . . . when I came out with it, black this black that, it was like I couldn't stop. I knew I had gone too far when even Mum was telling me to shut my trap, which as a matter wasn't making much sense at the time. But I couldn't help myself.

Denise   You couldn't?

Carly   Oh have a day off, Denise. But it wasn't him sitting there, looking all gorgeous and that, that clinched it with me and him. It was boxing! I don't know why that was but it always something I was serious with. Half-naked men.

Denise   Black men . . . don't forget that little component.

Carly   No . . . no . . . it's not . . . it's . . . well . . . no it's men getting all agile with each other.

Denise   Yeah right /

Carly   Alright maybe it's a factor, their skin glistening in the light /

Denise   See /

Carly   All athletic . . . as they prance around the ring, before they proceed to batter the life, it was like foreplay, followed by proper hot sex!

Denise   Enough now.

Carly   We all have our kinks, don't we?

Denise   . . .

Carly   Don't we? . . . (*To an audience member.*) Yeah I can see you do . . . especially you . . . you, mate . . . you . . . ain't fooling no one with that jacket . . . yeah . . . whether we like to admit it or not, boxing was mine, you don't like it, shove it.

Denise   You mind I don't shove you, hard!

Carly   Anyhow's, Michael, the lifelong chairperson of the I love Delroy Tomlin fan club, was going on about Delroy was a boxer, rising up through the junior amateur ranks, his next fight was up against Eddie Greg, who could not stop let alone would not stop trying to put his hand up my skirt at school. Music to my ears when Michael informed us Delroy was fighting him in the ring, and it was a joy to behold to see Delroy taking just one round to batter the living out of him. Uppercut, uppercut, jab, jab, and the sweetest of knockouts.

Denise (*proud*)   Mmmm, my boy that!

Carly   Eddie Greg wasn't doing or saying much by then, just eating the canvas. Dad was yelling with pride. Which was funny cos, Dad didn't like blacks, but he was screaming like a bleeding banshee for Delroy, who couldn't be any more black.

(*To an audience member.*) Confused? I was.

Shakes her head.

White people! Mum was going off as well. She loved her boxing as well as me . . . which now makes me wonder if . . . anyway . . . She could see that I was made up for Delroy, and in spite of my efforts, I had feelings for the twat. That was when, on the way home she took me aside and said the strangest, yet incredible thing ever to me.

Maggie   'So, tell me about Delroy?'

Carly   She enquired, trying to look nonchalant but coming off like the Gestapo.

'I don't know what you mean, Mum?'

Then she leaned into me, let her hair fall over one eye and . . .

Maggie   'Is he your "Avalon"?'

Carly   'My what?'

Maggie   '"Avalon"!'

Carly   She repeated and then quickly checked the room like a crow looks up from a carcass it's eating . . .

'I don't get it, Mum, what are you saying?'

Maggie   'When me and your dad were courting . . .'

Carly   'Courting?'

Maggie   'Yes courting, now listen, fingers on lips.'

Carly   Her face warming, her voice softening . . . her dimples framing a naughty grin.

Maggie   'On our second date he took me to out to a disco.'

Carly (*laughs again*)   'A disco!'

Maggie   'Do you want a slap?'

Carly   'No, Mum.'

Maggie   'DJ was playing all of the slow songs at the end. One of them was "Avalon" by Roxy Music. Your dad took me in his arms, and we danced . . . what felt like all night.'

Carly (*teases*)   'Oh yeah?'

Her eye's high in the left corner of its socket . . . as she beat time and relived the moment.

Maggie   'We had our first kiss. That was when I knew he was all mine, that I was going to spend the rest of my life with the twat. All of my mates, my entire family, warned me about him but I didn't care. He was my . . .'

Carly   '. . . "Avalon"?'

Maggie   'Well, come on then, big mouth, is Delroy yours?'

Carly   'I only like him, Mum.'

Her eyes widened but I couldn't read them, so I panicked.

'I just want to get off with him . . . to see what it's like with one of 'em.'

Maggie   'I'll pretend I didn't hear that.'

Carly   'You bloody asked!'

Maggie   'Don't mean I wanna answer.'

Carly   'You're like a episode of *Lost* you are . . . fucking mystery.'

Maggie   'Look, sweetheart, I just want you to be careful. If your dad saw what I saw between you and him.'

Carly   'All of those things he says about black people, Mum? Do you agree with him?'

Maggie   'Some of it, not all of it.'

Carly   She said, looking mystified by her own answer.

'You should have a word with him then.'

Maggie   'Carly, it's complicated.'

Carly   'But he listens to you, Mum, he might stop.'

Maggie   'I can't change who he is.'

Carly   'So you just shut up and ignore it?'

I said as though I was spitting rhymes at a rap battle.

Maggie   'Oi, watch yourself.'

Carly   But I didn't watch myself . . . I went in.

'I know he's my dad, but how can you love someone who thinks that way about other people?'

Maggie   'Not all people, just black people.'

Carly   'Oh that's alright then.'

Maggie   'Carly!'

Carly   'But how do you hold . . . kiss . . . make love with someone that you . . . fink is /'

Maggie   'Oi, we are discussing you, young lady, not me.'

Carly   I'd stung her, pricked her with my poison, so I pulled back . . . as the floor beneath me began to shake.

'I don't get it, Mum.'

Maggie   'Love, Carly, is a weird kind of . . . fing. It makes you do crazy things. It doesn't play fair, it makes no bleeding sense. I don't care who you are or what you do, it will always rise to the surface and find its way out, always. You can love all of a person, every cell in their body, and still not like some of what they say and what they do.'

Carly   'But it's fundamental . . . it's /'

Maggie   'Your dad is my "Avalon", Carly, that is all there is to it. We walk through this world together, me and him. And if you ever feel the same about Delroy, if one day he becomes your "Avalon" . . .'

Carly   'Mum! Fuck Dad! Fuck "Avalon"!'

And that was it. After giving me a slap round the head for swearing at her, we didn't say anything more about it, not for a long time. 'Avalon', I mean come the fuck on!

Denise   Burns me to say but I'm with you on that one.

Carly (*a little shocked*)   You are?

Denise   I mean, anyone with an egg cup of sense and a half decent taste in music would have told yer mum, 'Avalon' is not Roxy Music's finest hour. 'Slave to Love' however, that is their best tune to fall in love with, by far!

Carly   But I couldn't be in love with Delroy, at least that is what I was telling myself. But it didn't mean I couldn't have some fun with him. I goes to him, after he won the fight, I whispered to Delroy, in my sexiest Marilyn Monroe voice, that I could find.

Denise   Dutty gal.

Carly   'Well done, I'll thank you later.'

Denise   Dutty gal!

Carly   Yes thank you, Denise. I think they've all got it by now.

Sound of cheering. It is loud.

What was that? Did someone score? United?

Denise   You call yourself a Leyton girl?

Carly   Back off.

Denise   Think it through, nuh? You think it would be that loud if United scored?

Carly   Bloody Orient?

Denise (*confirms after listening to the radio*)   Yes, girl!

Carly   Bloody hell. Michael and Delroy must have
screamed their lungs out by now.

Denise   Speaking of which.

Carly   Right! Yeah, as I was saying, the look on Delroy's
boat race when I said what I said to him. He had no clue of
what I was talking about. Well, of course he didn't cos you
see, up until that point, I had no idea how Delroy felt about
me, I mean what was he into? I knew he liked the So Solid
ting. Lisa Maffia? Maybe Alesha Dixon? Jamelia with them
legs? So maybe white girls weren't his thing . . . he was one of
those brothers who preferred to keep it local?

Denise   I wish.

Carly   Can't say I blame him if that was the case, black don't
crack. Right?

I wanted to know what flicks his switch. I needed to find out,
he weren't going anywhere until I knew, I had it planned. I
was going all *Mission Impossible* on this. Spying on him,
finding out which gate from school did he leave from to go
home.

What bus home he took, did he do anything like play
basketball with his brers under the motorway like most of
them do, but most importantly was there a quiet spot for me
to face him, I mean there is no point in doing any of this if
we cannot find a little moment to have some, you know, QT
together. It took me weeks to figure it all out. I knew all
about his short walk down Regis Road just after he got off
the bus, I also knew about a quiet alleyway on that road. I
decided to arm myself. I was stacked, I was in.

Off came the school uniform. On went a tight Lycra top, and
a pair of them tight jogging pants that I borrowed off my
sister Lisa. Oh yes, Delroy was my mission, should I choose
to accept it. Of course I bloody did. Totally lost for words
when he catches sight of me and then I produced, 'I hear
once you go black, you never go back.'

(*To audience.*) I know! Then I planted a kiss on him, one of my finest, before he has the chance to say anything. But it was the feeling I had when he kissed me back, the way he stared at me. The way he held me. So determined, and strong, like he wouldn't let go.

I could smell him on me for days. I could feel the touch of our lips together whenever I shut my eyes. It was beautiful. It was bliss. I thought to myself, fucking hell, Mum was right. Delroy's my 'Avalon'.

Denise   Really?

Carly   He bloody is, Denise. He always will be. He knew it. I knew it. We still know it. He was my first, you know?

Denise (*does not believe*)   Like fuck!

Carly   And I was his first!

Denise   You expect me to believe . . .

Carly   Believe what you like. It's true, Dee. When we finally did it . . .

Denise   *Did it?*

Carly   It meant something, for us both, it was something special.

Denise   Just before you had him hiding under your bed when your dad came home.

Carly   He will always be my 'Avalon', Dee.

Denise   Oh for Christ . . . he is sleeping on the *bloody* sofa, Carly.

Carly   I've got some breaking news for you, Denise. I am the one sleeping on our *bloody* sofa.

Denise   You?

Carly   Yeah, I thought that'll rock your world.

Denise   How very modern of you and very unchivalrous of him.

Carly   He said at first, he'd do it. I told him, well, screamed more like, that I'll sleep on the sodding sofa if that is how he bloody well feels.

Denise   Huh!

Carly   I never thought he'd take me up on it. So go on, piss yourself laughing, why don't you?

Denise   Laughing? We're all gonna be paying off our debts long after this place turns into 'GAIL'S'. I ain't laughing.

Carly   He said he couldn't bear to look at me, he still can't. Whenever I step into a room, he walks out.

Denise   You fucked that up, didn't yer?

Carly   He'll forgive me, if Orient win today.

Denise   *If* being the operative word. Wake up, girl.

Carly   Cos I tell you, *girl*, every time Orient win, Delroy's libido goes up a notch. You have no idea.

Denise   Do you mind?

Carly   It's my only chance at this rate.

Denise   Don't be so quick to believe yer own shit. He heard it as well. You and that mouth. That mouth!

Carly   I know what I said, I know what me and my *dutty* mouth did, ok. Am I ever going to hear the end of it?

Denise (*points to the shop*)   Take a good look, Carly. This is the end of it.

Carly   I can't keep doing this, Denise.

Denise   As soon as this man shows, we hand over the keys, you won't have to. We're done.

Carly   Do you want a cup of tea?

Denise What?

Carly Yes or no?

Denise You're asking if I want tea?

Carly Yes Denise, cos I am a nice person, it has been known. I need a break.

(*Gestures to the audience.*) You talk to them for a bit, rinse the fuck out of me to them, why don't yer? Tell them summin, go on.

She goes inside.

Scene Three

Denise (*to the audience*)   It was a thing being so meshed with her . . . yes cos Carly's my daughter in sin . . . and now a business partner and . . . well . . . I heard someone say don't be with someone who you just love, that love ain't enough, that you can love lots a partners but there's only a few you can build a life with . . . be with someone who you can be a life partner to . . . grow with. So whilst I know I could never love Carly instantly especially with that voice of hers . . . and we weren't in that kind of relationship, I did, however, feel like we had a future . . . even if I had to watch my son turn into a nodding dog around her . . . and her kinda of whiteness . . . can I say that . . . let's say 'lens', so no one gets triggered . . . her kinda of 'lens' was a challenge . . . she is, however, I hate to say it, kinda good for him. And she had given me Meghan . . . oh you didn't know? Yeah they went and named their baby Meghan, yeah I know, don't, please just don't. I'm not sure if they was being nouveau riche or nouveau radical . . . but, anyways, Meghan is the best thing that has ever happened to me. So you gotta roll with it . . . right? And bwoy sometimes we rolled . . . let me tell ya.

Carly *walks back out with two mugs and a bottle of Prosecco.*

Carly Still 1–0?

Denise   Still 1–0.

Carly   United will equalise.

Denise   Most likely.

Carly   At least we're still in it then.

Denise   You could say that . . . or you could say nearly out of it . . . Can you imagine the amount of batty flapping if it went to penalties?

Carly (*points to audience*)   Has she been saying something? 'bout me?

Denise   Why would I be saying anything?

Carly   So, what you doing being so nice to me for? /

Denise   Oh behave yourself /

Carly   You're being /

Denise   I ain't /

Carly   You rinsing me again? To them?

Denise   You told me to.

Carly   I suggested.

Denise (*pointing to Prosecco*)   What's that?

Carly   What's it look like?

Denise   You said tea.

Carly   I know what I said but I found this bottle inside. It must have been a leftover from the grand opening.

Denise   How ironic.

Carly   I thought we could drown our sorrows. Do it proper. Fancy it?

Denise   Bit early.

Carly   Dee . . . I work . . . well . . . 'worked' with you.

She takes it as they look at each other knowingly.

Denise   Ok, I have been known to enjoy a glass /

Carly   Bottle or three more like. Joke! Well, carry on then, say what you have to say to them, don't let me stop you.

Denise   I was saying how well we worked together.

Carly *laughs hard.*

Carly   Oh yeah this I gotta hear . . . gwan den.

Denise   Oh so . . . you're woman enough to take it.

Carly   With a drink in my hand, yeah.

She opens the bottle.

Maybe it's a good thing I got a bottle.

Denise   Cool . . . ok . . . You remember 'space-gate'?

Carly   What are you on about?

Denise   Allow me to refresh.

(*To the audience.*) So this gal, right . . . we're a couple of months in and I'm making some p's . . . not rice and peas . . . paper money p's yeah . . . and she's . . . well . . . flowers are going down like . . . like the Queen's Jubilee in Barbados . . . people be like, 'Flowers! I can't pay my rent' . . . so people are seeing me as presenting a better option for their money, right?

A full belly . . . you can't compete in a recession. Especially as they see my patties are filled . . . not the pastry filled with air, like most patties but made with low-raising pastry, so what you see is what you're eating . . . basically, I got a queue and she ain't.

Carly   That's not fair . . . I didn't mean /

Denise   Can I tell it or what /

Carly   I did not mean /

Denise   Well, let's see what they think . . . right? Not talking what you 'meant', I'm chatting what happened . . . white women always chatting 'bout what they meant or mean . . . like a we don't understand the law.

Carly   I'm white women now . . . already . . . two sups of that and I'm white women.

Denise   Going on like we don't know . . . 'I didn't mean' if you don't mean to drive at 33 miles an hour down a 20-mile-an-hour road, its still an offence you know.

Carly   Denise!

Denise   I'm sorry I don't mean it like dat . . . against you . . . I like you . . . look can I tell it how I see it, without you telling me how I should say it . . . just once . . . I may see things badly but . . . . You might understand what I see . . . even 'if' you disagree . . . you might really 'know' what you disagree with, if you shut your 'ole fi two secs. So we're in the shop one morning and . . .

'Awww awww awww awww aww.'

Carly   'What you done?'

Denise   She spat across the room /

'Bun up me hand pon de bludclaart ting . . . Shit!'

Carly   'Do you mind?'

Denise   Now . . . remember this is me . . . Denise. I don't ball for much . . . I've been known to pick a fight with Millwall fans for shouting too loudly on the 58 bus . . . feel me.

'Awww, FUCK!'

Carly   'Denise . . . I got a customer.'

Denise   'Me look like I give a sunflower-shaped fuck . . . I'm in pain . . . can't you help?'

Carly   'Oh great she's gone, thanks, Denise, that was my first and only customer all morning.'

Denise   'Look . . . look at my hand.'

Still trying to elicit some empathy from her, which was akin to Russians trying to get worldwide internet access under that bludclaart Putin.

Carly   'Next time can you /'

Denise   'Burn in silence?'

Carly   'How about not . . . just not burning your /'

Denise   'I didn't wake up this morning thinking a third-degree burn across my metacarpals would spice up my day, Carly.'

I said, wishing I had a pitchfork to juke her with.

Carly   'Water . . . put it under the fucking tap then.'

Denise   I did just that, I put my hand under the tap. Holding down my tears as I wanted her to know how angry I was with her . . . but it didn't work as what felt like a golf ball-sized tear slalomed down my face.

Carly   'Oh and another thing, babe . . . your music.'

Denise   'My music?'

Carly   'Loud . . . it's too bleeding loud, Denise /'

Denise   'Loud /'

Carly   'Ish /'

Denise   'Loud or loudish?'

I enquired with a pincer-like focus. See what she didn't know is black people and their music is, well, actually maybe I should say white people and their silence is . . . and black people and their music . . . no . . . what am I trying to say . . . it's like who owns what? We know who owns this land . . . white people, we have to swallow dat . . . colonialism is a bitch . . . but the airwaves?

Airwaves is something we all own, right? And we . . . as in black people, love fe dominate it . . . and sometimes it's as a reaction to . . . it's like a provocation . . . it's like you wanna own dat as well?! It's a thing that the Europeans can't take from us and so it's become that . . . we love to make up noise . . . music . . . it's the soundtrack of defiance, of rebellion, of justice and, well, it's become part of our culture . . . so . . . when anyone, especially a facety lickle white gyal . . . with her hair scraped back, rocking a Dax hair gel look, teefing a black gyal look, coming like she's knows we . . . turns round and says 'turn down your music' . . . it feels like you are literally talking to my ancestors and telling them they can't speak Swahili on the plantation . . . now I ain't saying it's fair . . . I just telling you what it is.

Denise   'Loud or loudish?'

Carly   'Loud . . . it's too bloody loud for a florist . . . I feel like I'm down Fabric waiting for someone to spill yet another rum and coke down my back.'

Denise   'Oh really?'

Carly   'Yeah.'

Denise   'Is it now?'

. . . as I put down my bale of cotton and looked to my ancestors.

Carly   'I get that you got vibes and ting going but that coupled with the smell /'

Denise   'Smell?'

I said disguising the hurricane brewing with a high-pitched politeness . . . I then repeated it for effect alone . . .

'Smell?'

Carly   'Yeah but I'll let that go'

Denise   . . . she said seemingly oblivious.

'Let that go? /'

Carly 'Yeah cos . . . cos well, you're cooking /'

Denise 'Dat's right /'

Carly 'But oh my days . . . you got more beats per day than a metalhead's all-nighter.'

Denise 'You finish?'

Carly 'What . . . yeah . . . I guess.'

'Good, cos me ah talk now.'

I said as though I was direct descendant of Haile bludclaart Selassie I!

'See now I never complained 'bout your dirty van blocking the door while you and Michael argue loudly about the highest-level trivia you can possibly argue about, whilst bringing in a 'manure'-smelling delivery . . . or the way that 'Emporium' woman's nose turns up at the sight of my black customers when she buys her weekly 'Ladies Fingers' for her overpriced minimalist rip-off 'antique' furniture shop . . . do I? No?

'Because we're trying a ting together . . . I don't moan when literally first thing in the morning, you come tell me about some poor black girl being molested by a white policeman at school . . . and ask me what do I think? Squirting your virtue-signalling feminist white gal bullshit on me . . . Before I've even had a coffee . . . or even remembered I'm black and oppressed! Like it hurts you the same way it hurts me . . . but do I moan? . . . no . . . cos we trying a ting . . . we're evolving, I keep telling myself . . . did you ever think I was trying to tell you something about me with the tune I was playing? . . . or guide you into the mood I was in? . . . did you ever listen to the feel of it? . . . think that perhaps if you listened to the lyrics you may understand why it needs to be bludclaart loud!

'Encourage your customer to hear it . . . deeply . . . and that could . . . actually be a selling point for you.'

Carly   Yeah, yeah, yeah, and what did I do?

Denise   Don't look smug now cos you know where we ended up.

Carly   Moi.

Denise   But yeah . . . you came correct . . . eventually long time after some white girl tears did fill up the room.

Carly   Denise!

Denise   Come off it, you were throwing some right Amber Heard shapes.

Carly   Dee!

Denise   I thought you must have taken me for a man . . . one dem man that get hard when they see a woman cry . . . come on . . . we've all played that card on dem fool fool men . . . but yeah, yeah, yeah, eventually you did say:

Carly   'I don't . . . Denise . . . I don't do any of that . . . so let's do that?'

Denise   'You?'

I said not hiding one molecule of disbelief.

'You?'

Carly   'Yeah me, from now on I'll do that, Denise . . .'

Denise   'Eh?'

'Yeah and I promise I won't say some upsetting shit to you first thing in the morning again to start your day.'

I couldn't believe it . . . you just switched you shit there and then. We started doing deals on stuff together . . . sharing costs . . . sharing ideas. Delroy and Michael couldn't fathom it could they . . . we even watched the fucking King's coronation together on TV . . . Remember? 'A shame that amount of people could not turn out for something /'

Delroy   'Mum /'

Denise   Delroy interrupted in a sly effort to divert dissent.

'What?'

I replied playfully.

Delroy   'Let them enjoy /'

Denise   'I not stopping anyone enjoying themselves . . . if they can really find eighty-two loud explosions emanating from a hundred-year-old cannon enjoyable? Then . . .'

Carly   'How 'bout the planes? /'

Denise   'Instruments of war? Enjoyable? Ok. While dressed in pantomime clothes and spending 100 million pounds of taxpayers' money . . . not their money, you know, our money.'

Dat's when the dial changed, feathers ruffled . . . necks started to get scratched, bwoy.

Michael   'But ain't it nice to see them all up there . . . the King's family . . . all that life lived as royals . . . it's /'

Denise   'What did she call 'em? . . . Working royals? So no paedos or blacks . . . perfect . . . just a wholesome clean living white military colonialist family.'

Delroy   'Why you gotta do this? . . . we're in '23 not '83.'

Denise   Delroy squeezed out a tight jaw.

Carly   'Don't do that, Delroy.'

Delroy   'Eh?'

Carly   'That . . . where you try and make out that cos she's got a different opinion on it you can't enjoy it /'

Delroy   'I can't . . . I love those old fighter planes and stuff . . . rubber-faced Lionel Richie ain't that bad /'

Denise   All those years of watching *Law and Order* finally found a purpose.

'I put it to you.'

I said, clearing my throat . . . with the timing and rhythm of James Brown.

'You love the power it shows . . . so how come when Kim Yong Un had a 'show' of his military might, it was a 'disgusting display of power' . . . and when we show our mighty, long, history of military dominance, that lead to all the countries we colonised struggling for survival . . . with still no apology. It's divine . . . right? Ordained by God? A lovely show, for that family to remember the good old days. I mean how is it fun, to watch that old cadaverous, jumbo the elephant-eared, racist beanpole become a king?'

I know, I know, I know . . . I couldn't help it.

Delroy   'That's it, Mum!'

Denise   Delroy exclaimed as if his life depended on it.

Delroy   'They all have a history that means something to them . . . you can't come in here and try and make them /'

Denise   'They're a gangster family with the best fiction . . . mythology.'

Michael   'Oh come on /'

Denise   'Without the fig leaf of that little old lady, it's plain to see what they serve and it ain't God /'

Poor Michael, even with all his new-found liberalism, wanted to scream.

Delroy   'MUM . . . for fuck's sake /'

Denise   Delroy hollered . . . spitting his burger in his lap.

'What? We're from a colony, Delroy . . . what'dya expect me to fink /'

Delroy   'Slavery is over, let them have their day /'

Denise   Hearing that from my own kin sliced a main artery, weakening my poise.

'We only just stop paying the slave owners in the last decade for their loss of earnings . . . all we got is that they "tolerate" us /'

Michael   'Yeah but I . . . we . . . love the royal family, they give us a . . . a /'

Denise   'A sense that you're better than everyone else /'

Delroy   'Mum!'

Denise   Delroy pleaded now standing and breathing heavy.

'You watch . . . Caribbean people won't have no man waving his dick in their face /'

Michael   'That's it! For /'

Carly   'See it from her perspective? . . . why not? . . . eh?!'

Denise   Piped in Carly. Should have seen their face . . . it was as if they'd seen a six-foot lizard, in a shirt and tie, eating a curry on the M25.

Delroy   'Cos, cos, cos, it's a celebration.'

Denise   'Of?'

Delroy   'The beginning of his rule.'

Denise   'Over?'

Delroy   'His country.'

Denise   'And?'

Delroy   'I don't /'

Denise   'His colonies . . . over his colonies . . . Delroy, don't act like you don't understand.'

Delroy   'I just didn't want to mash up the fucking holiday . . . their frigging holiday.'

Denise   He offered desperately trying to hold his adult form . . . and failing badly.

Delroy   'We're on holiday . . . it's a bank holiday . . . street party, drinks, celebration, you know . . . even me, I can choose to forget the . . . erm, 'nuances' of it . . . for a few flipping days.'

Commentator   'Him who liveth and reigneth supreme, over all things'

Denise   I goes . . .

'Where's the fucking nuance in that, Delroy!'

I said, pointing to the TV.

'A seventy-four-year-old man who's never worked a day in his life is being showered from head to toe with a billion quids worth of stolen bling. Not much fucking nuance there. I swear allegiance to His Majesty, mi boomba! I pay my tax. That should be allegiance enough for dem claarts!'

I'd torn it . . . no punctured it . . . could almost hear the sound of it leaving the room like a dry heavy fart.

Then Carly . . . yeah Carly cut through the room with.

Carly   'For fuck's sake you lot, will you all stop fiddling with your genitalia for one sec. We see the performative wank of 'aving a black choir singing and how a black deacon bowing and scraping to a man wearing the bling stolen from her ancestors looks . . . but how about we celebrate that we at least survived her rule, the Queen and that? . . . eh? Look at us . . . maybe they couldn't handle a mixed-race couple in their family, but we can . . . can't we? We can try, Denise, we can try . . . try and hold a complicated past and a vision of the present and future?. . . can't we? We can hold two ideas in our head without trying to shit on one of them? Can't we? We all just trying right? That's it . . . let's celebrate trying? Let's celebrate that.

'Trying. Please?'

Denise   She done me . . . I . . . I . . . I . . . felt . . . felt hope, I
felt . . . (*She cries.*) like we could get a piece . . . I could get a
piece . . . of that . . . dream . . . that I had a chance . . . if I
just tried . . . if I just kept on trying . . . if I just keep trying
. . . and I thought of all those woman . . . black woman, that
had come through . . . broke through like a rose in concrete
gardens.

English black roses in a concrete garden . . . Brave, beautiful,
boundless talent. I felt them lifting me, I could smell hot
combs, cocoa butter, Vicks VapoRub, Dax, Luster pink oil
moisturiser . . . I could hear my dead mum telling me not to
give up . . . 'We don't give up, Denise, you is a Tomlin, never
give up.'

She done me, Carly done me, I saw it, finally saw what
Delroy was banging on about in full. Like we'd been getting
on, as I said, but . . . I hadn't seen the force of her, the . . .
she lit up the bloody room . . . like some beautiful luminous
sea creature plunging us all into darkness . . . and then she
come with.

Carly   'Ah, Denise, look at em, eh? Full of pomp and wealth
. . . bunch of blinged-up waxwork statues . . . eh what d'ya
fink of dis saying then, "Big blanket mek man sleep late."'

Denise   In perfect patois it was . . . and I had to laugh . . .
she made me laugh hard . . . can you fall in love with
someone, with one sentence . . . can you? Cos I did.

(*So proud.*) My daughter from another. That is what she
became. In the blink of an eye. I felt seen by her . . . I knew
she loved up the royals and dat but I felt seen . . . but that
was her downfall . . . She knew too much . . . she knew us . . .
but still wasn't us . . . so still didn't know enough.

Scene Four

A very inebriated **Carly** *on video, roaring with laughter.*

Carly   'Bloody hell, tell driver to . . . what's his name . . . Roger?'

Girl   'Tell us then . . . come on.'

Carly   'Alright, alright then, you bitches, listen up, shut yer cunts, I'll give it to yer. Five ways to keep yer black man, you ready? I say you ready?'

Girls   'Yeah! Yeah . . .'

Carly   'Alright, here they come. *Number one!* And this one is the most important of all. You must know all there is to know about a black man's . . .'

Girl   '. . . cock!'

Carly   'hair, hair, you dirty bitch! Listen, don't ever touch a black man's . . .'

Girls   'Big black ha ha ha.'

Carly   'hair, his hair, don't go near a black man's hair, unless you have a prior invitation. Listen . . . stop . . . what ya?

'. . . stop taking selfies and listen up . . . the morning of his cousin's wedding Delroy heads for his usual barbers up by Stratford East. The place is heaving. Del was in tears, he had not had his hair done in weeks, and already it was starting to look like whatever it is that was sitting on the head of Tina Turner!

'"I can't go to the wedding looking like this."

'Bawling like a fucking newborn he was. Making more noise than Meghan did when she popped herself out of me. All nine and half pounds of her. At that point, I got out my clippers that I bought on Amazon for this very reason, sat him down. Now, your man is going to be looking at you like you just took a shit in front of his grandparents who have

never missed a Sunday church visit since they stepped off
the Empire *Windrush*! But stay strong. Hold your nerve.
Hold his head ask him summin like . . . Do you want yer
usual line in the back with fade? Yeah? . . . but keep it longer
on the top?

'When he nods, with a sense of panic, yer in girl! . . . oh shit
. . . might 'ave to take these off . . . right. So . . . You have got
it all to play for. Just keep coming out with it, like yer
chatting sense, the detailers, talk about his hairline . . . How
many centimetres do you want off the top babe, one, one
and half, two?

'By then, he'll name it for you. It's all about the medium
fade, low fade, zero fade, with them brothers. When he
knows what he wants, you had better know what do with
those clippers. Blurry waves, deep waves, a sweet-looking
360. A short side and a burst. Learn that shit up. And when
yer done, when he checks himself in the mirror and sees
how crisp he looks, thanks to your fine-looking white self,
he'll be yours forever, girl!'

Girl   'Yer a black man's mattress! Ha ha ha . . .'

Carly   'Number 2.'

Girls   '. . . Number two, number two!'

Carly   'Make him feel loved. Tell him, over and over, you
understand, that you know he is a black man living in a white
world and that you are with him, every step of the way with
that. So the next time you are on a train with him and some
white woman clutches her bag like we do, especially you.

'Whenever a black brer sits next to us,'

Girls   'No I don't . . . yeah you do, ha ha ha ha.'

Carly   'Well, feel free to give that bitch one of yer fierce
looks like yer saying . . .

'Don't mek my man feel like that, is who are you? . . . Don't
get . . . your face, ha ha.'

'Yeah mek him feel loved, so don't get vex every time he turns up fucking late for everything! I know, don't get me started, it stirs my pot something chronic. How hard is it to show up on time?

'They have no concept of it, it's black man time for them, you just have to accept it and move on. Try being late a few times yourself, revenge is sweet . . . It will become a habit.

'Number three. Don't just tell him that you love hip hop. You gotta show him you love hip hop. You gotta quote the best hardcore rappers there is, one of his favourites that he knows off by heart. Snoop, Kanye, Nas . . . no, no Public Enemy!

(*Raps.*)
    Elvis was a hero to most
    But he, Elvis was a hero to most Elvis was a hero to most
    But he never meant shit to me, you see,
    Straight up racist that sucker was
    Simple and plain.
    Motherfuck him and John Wayne.
    Cause I'm black and I'm proud.
    I'm ready and hyped plus I'm amped
    Most of my heroes don't appear on no stamps.

'See? Nuttin' to it . . . watch how his nostril flair with lust . . .

'Number four. Pretend you like his food or should I say his mum's food.

'They spice everything.'

Girl   'Yeah it's too spicy.'

Carly   'Yeah and if it ain't some tongue-piercing hot sauce, it's some over-salted jerk shit . . . salt, babe, they love to put on everything they eat . . . and wonder why they get high blood pressure.

'Well, good luck with that I say . . .'

Car swerves.

'Oi, oi, oi . . . give Roger another bump will yer, he's driving like Stevie Wonder. But anyway to keep your man . . . buy yourself a West Indian cookbook, Levi Roots or somebody, and learn a recipe . . . ackee or bleeding saltfish, shit like that. He will love you up big time if you tell him you went on some bus trek to Brixton fucking market or bleeding Hackney to find these ingredients, when truth is, get them in cans from your nearest Asda.

'Number five. Express yourself to his entire tribe! Driver! Roger! Is it? Yeah . . . can I . . . can I have the aux? Is it bluetooth? Thanks, yeah . . .'

She plays Candy.

'Delroy took me to his cousin's wedding. He warned me beforehand I'd be the 'only white gal there', and they might do this at the reception. I had his cousins and aunties all glaring at me, they all feel a way about white gals like me taking their men. Who think they have better rhythm! This is your moment. That was my time.'

Carly *performs the Candy dance. She is a natural.*

'Two steps to the right, tap with yer left, go to the left, one, two, tap on yer right. Go back . . . slide, oh yes! I'd been practising for weeks. I had it down. I was on it! I was fire! A sexy lowdown twerk at the end, but hey if you have it, why not flaunt it? I couldn't wait to flick my 'real' hair in the face of the first one of them bad gals who gave me the eye. I was ready to lift up my dress, thrust my pussy to all a dem, and in my best Denise patwa say, 'See it deh, smell it nuh! kiss me hole' . . . ha, ha, ha, jokes jokes but yeah get me.

'Once they are done gawping at you, you tek yer man and you march him off, making sure everyone of them can see. Watch how they turn green with envy! It go eat them up, enjoy! By now, you more than earned that shit. As soon as you get him alone, your place or his, don't matter, his shirt and boxers should be ripped right the fuck off him in less than a minute. He should be on his knees, seeing to you down below. Tell him that feels great, 'dat's my boy', tell him to go slow, then fast, then slow, whatever flicks your switch, babe, dem black brothers like nuttin better than to be told what to do by sum man-hungry snow bunny on heat. Tek advantage of that.'

Scene Five

Denise   When I saw that /

Carly   I didn't /

Denise   When I saw you . . . like that, drunk like that /

Carly   I didn't think /

Denise   It was like you were going full throttle Fletcher on me.

Carly   No, don't.

Denise   Just like your dad and your brother.

Carly (*pleads*)   Stop it.

Denise   I honestly felt I just didn't know you.

Carly   Denise /

Denise   I lost all sight of you . . . but it was you.

Carly   Dee /

Denise   Same hair, same voice, same everything . . . just all the words coming out of your mouth like some tourist /

Carly   Denise /

Denise   Dat's what we'd call white men who just wanted to taste black, so he could say before he'd died, he had one of us.

Carly   Tourist? /

Denise   Yes, Carly, a tourist /

Carly Wow /

Denise I don't know if it is to just satisfy their racism barometer or what, but that's what we called them /

Carly Me? /

Denise Yeah, you . . . You came off like one of dem deh people. A fucking tourist! With my son . . . mugging off my son . . . mugging off me, women . . . black women.

Carly I'm a feminist, I'm down for all women you know dat. It was a sodding hen party, I was off my face.

Denise Oh, no, no, no, don't please talk about your white feminism . . . aywhda rass is up with you and dat man?

All women, yeah? . . . Ukrainian women gets flung out of their country . . . 'Oh, maybe we should look into trying to help them', yeah, put them up, make space . . . look how many black and brown women are refugees and no desire, no policy, no money to look after them . . . None of you give a fuck about those 'women' . . . send them off to Rwanda.

Carly I'm not no politician . . . why you always making out like we not the same when we are really /

Denise Ok . . . at the hen do . . . that you was at . . . spouting ya five ways to keep a black man. How many black women where there, Carly?

Carly None.

Denise But we the same?

Carly It wasn't my hen night.

Denise How many at your birthday drinks last year?

Carly . . .

Denise At Meghan's christening? That I didn't bring?

Carly . . .

Denise At your New Year's party?

Carly   . . . a few actually . . . no, no /

Denise   At 'your' baby shower?

Carly   . . .

Denise   And you have a black man and a black daughter.

Carly   . . .

Denise   So don't talk to me about feminism . . . till you talk about it to all women . . . yeah? Don't open your fucking mouth about any of it . . . till you heard from all women . . . listen to all women.

Silence.

Carly   Bet you loved it when you saw it? /

Denise   Really? /

Carly   Right? /

Denise   Don't /

Carly   Bet it filled you up, innit?

Denise   What? /

Carly   Bet you was sated for real /

Denise   Don't be stupid /

Carly   Yeah, right /

Denise   We're partners how could I be /

Carly   Proved you right though?

Denise   Don't chat /

Carly   Never liked me from the off /

Denise   But like I said you grew on me /

Carly   Like fungus.

Denise   Come on /

Carly   Bet you forwarded the fuck out of it.

Denise   We lost our business because of that . . . why would I?

Carly   Cos deep down you hate me . . . us . . . and maybe you should . . . I'm not good enough for your son, you're right /

Denise   You wanna know what else happened when I first saw it /

Carly   No . . . no . . . I bloody don't thanks . . .

Denise   Let me /

Carly   Sod that . . . no bloody way.

Denise   Carly, you might /

Carly   No . . . boo hoo, poor you . . . you got triggered . . . I KNOW! Ok . . . I fucked it /

Denise   No you don't know . . .

Carly   I'm a cunt /

Denise   CARLY /

Carly   I know ok . . . I know! Michael told me already . . . 'Your mouth could turn a Buddhist monk into Fred West, Carly' . . . I know!

Denise   Why'd do you always think you know? . . . I AM NOT LIKE YOU! Or Michael or Delroy, I'm me.

Carly   I said sorry! I went online and said sorry /

Denise   Ha ha ha /

Carly   Don't laugh like that, I did!

Denise   I know you did /

Carly   Well, don't /

Denise   I don't wanna talk about that /

Carly   Typical.

Denise   What is typical is you?

Carly   Oh tell me do.

Denise   You typically . . . don't wanna hear what actually happened when I saw it.

Carly   You said already /

Denise   I said what I felt.

Carly   Oh right.

Denise   Not what happened.

Beat.

Carly   Fucking go on then . . . torture you are, like fucking torture . . . you should join the fucking Taliban . . . Learn a trick or two off you they could.

Denise   I've gone round to see mi cousin, Cynthia . . . she'd jus reach back from JA . . . and we're there in her kitchen . . . oh and my girl Jules was there too, Jules who somehow, and I'm not sure how, has become closer to Cynthia than me. But that's another story . . . so we there . . . me Cynthia and frigging Jules . . . all looking as though we'd spent three months wages on our hair . . . and, of course, a glass of Prosecco in hand.

Cynthia   'Ting bus open inna de suitcase and now me knickers smell like Wray and Nephew.'

Denise   Cynthia bellowed, trying as hard as she could to expose her sun-kissed skin.

Jules   'White rum?'

Denise   Jules chimed in with, 'over'-empathically.

Cynthia   'Yeah.'

Denise   'Na you say . . . your lady parts could intoxicate a man?'

Cynthia   'Not because of its smell.'

Denise   We laughed, like old friends at a Magic Mike show, as she guiltily unloaded the goodies from the suitcase onto the kitchen table.

'So what you saying? Auntie never send me back a rum?'

Cynthia   'You can buy it here you know.'

Denise   'That's not what me ask you.'

Jules   'You in trouble now . . .'

Denise   Jules poked, already breaking open a packet of bammy.

Cynthia   'Dee, she can't remember where her teeth are now, much less remember to buy you rum.'

Denise   'Really /'

Cynthia   'Here, have a mango.'

Denise   'No pear?'

Cynthia   'Bwoy, man . . . why do we have to turn into a Jamaican produce shop every bloody holiday?'

Denise   'To show we care.'

She then unveiled the largest pear . . . advocado to you . . . that you ever seen. Kissed her teeth and smiled at the same time . . . which ain't easy . . . and rested it slowly in my hand . . . A victorious grin washed over my face . . . then.

Jules   'Erm, Dee . . . is . . . is this your.'

Jules *raises her phone up.*

'Lord ah God . . . a what di.'

'What?

My jaw slacked! Exposing my cracked bottom teeth.

Jules   'Delroy's . . . can't be . . . oh my days . . . is, is, is this, Carly?'

Denise   Now you'd think eyes would be the giveaway but nope . . . it was the way her leg started to shake as if she'd just been electrocuted. She played it for us all to hear . . .

Cynthia . . . took back the pear quicktime. And rest just stood up and stared a me as though I'd said it. I . . . had sanctioned it . . . or penned it for you to say.

'What's she on? . . . She must be drunk bad.'

Cynthia   'Drunk?! That's one racist renk bitch deh, bwoy.'

Denise   She screeched, folding her arms so tightly I'm surprised she could breathe.

'Wait till I have words with her?'

Cynthia   'What?'

Denise   'It woulda ave a be some kinda joke gone bad /'

Cynthia   'Joke gone bad . . . You mad!'

Jules   'Yeah, look at her with her gang.'

Denise   Jules's eyebrows lifted so high . . . they hid under the hairline of her weave.

Jules   'Laughing their heads off at us . . . yeah, we the joke.'

Denise   'It's not us it, it, it, it's . . . fuck what's she under . . . she might be on drugs you know, Charlie or something.'

I said as I watched my life flying away like a child watches their first helium ballon disappearing in the sky and then exploding.

Cynthia   'Dat makes it wash, Charlie is that the best you got? . . . about no concept of time . . .'

Denise   'Delroy is always late /'

Cynthia 'My dad had a very good concept of time, every day working for forty-five rass years for the NHS.'

Jules 'My brother hates being late /'

Cynthia 'Innit . . . or my dad would have been sacked innit /'

Jules 'Facety lickle . . . lickle lickle.'

Denise Julie's speech stifled by anger . . . her eyes bright with rage.

Cynthia 'How could he end up with dat white . . . white . . . skank.'

There it was . . . the my 'sell out son' line . . . she didn't say it but that's what she meant . . . we all knew it and whilst I disagreed with that, in my head, my heart agreed. 'I said I will talk to her . . . don't be cussing her like dat. She's alright, she just /'

Jules 'Oh you switch . . . before it was piss head dis . . . trash dat . . . now you making monies together it's oh let me talk to her.'

Denise Luckily my left earlobe needed rubbing . . . but it could not hide my shame.

Cynthia 'Everybody switch when there's a buck to be earned, innit.'

Denise Cynthia presented as if the eleventh bludclaart holy commandment.

Jules 'Did you hear that?! We can smell her pussy . . . wha?!'

Cynthia 'Yeah it's disgusting.'

Denise 'She got it from me.'

Cynthia 'Say?'

Denise 'Like I get it from you.'

Cynthia   'Chat shit.'

Denise   'Cynthia, I have heard you say "Go kiss me hole" to man nuff times.'

Cynthia   'When I'm vex . . . cha dat's different /'

Jules   'Dat shit about only salty food . . . what?'

Denise   Jules proclaimed somehow throughly baffled by the notion.

Jules   'I mean . . . how . . . what planet? . . . The only tasty British food is fried and salted . . . fish and chips and that ain't even British!'

Denise   They all vibed. Even her cat D'angelo seem to nod in agreement.

'I know . . . I remember when they used to boil everything till it was as limp as their hair.'

I said, trying to stay on side . . . but I got nothing . . . no vibe to be found.

'Only when dem start look at how we cook, Indian man cook . . . Italian man cook, them start to come correct . . . I know, I know man . . . I know.'

I petered out aimlessly. All I could think about was wanting to kill Carly with my bare hands for putting me in this. And all the yard food mi cook for that woman, too! When she had all of that morning sickness, muggins here was the one who made her a nice drink of soursop to calm her stomach and fill her up with vitamins. A splash of the lime, and some coconut milk, a little sprinkle of nutmeg, juice of a lemon.

When it comes to prepping soursop, I can't be touched.

Jules   'And about she go flick her *real* hair in our face.'

Cynthia   'Well, she can't talk to me cos this is my hair.'

Jules   'Well, *this* ain't, 'bout she cussin' my weave. Facety bitch!'

Cynthia   'And go tell her dis . . . the black men I date . . . don't need to be told what to do.'

Jules   'Tinks if you tef our culture then that makes you alright.'

Cynthia   'Rude and racist.'

Denise   'She ain't racist /'

Cynthia   'So what she?'

Denise   I coughed trying to buy time.

'This family, bwoy, why Delroy have befriend and date dis blasted family /'

Jules   'Yeah, Michael's a spanner too.'

Denise   'How you know Michael?'

Jules   'Oh I met him at . . . at . . . at erm . . . some club . . . night before his dad's funeral, and then we . . . doesn't matter . . . Him a spanner.'

Denise   She said, clearly hiding something juicy. But I knew she'd never say.

'All of dem is trouble, bwoy . . . why dem?'

Cynthia   'Because you failed him /'

Denise   'Oh . . . how? Go on . . . come wid it, how?'

I said ready to pull both her fake and real nails off for an answer.

Cynthia   'I don't /'

Denise   'Me? How? . . . How did I fail him?'

My bottom lip now bending out of shape in upset /

'How?'

Silence.

Cynthia   'I don't mean dat . . . I don't . . . I'm sorry.'

Denise   'So you say things you don't mean?'

The question floated in the air as dandelion do in summer.

'Why we gotta always blame women? Blame . . . blame . . . always someone we want to blame.'

Jules   'Thought you should know it's gone viral . . . people talking boycotting your shop . . . a petition already.'

Denise   Jules's eyes wide with excitement.

'No . . . no . . . no.'

Jules   'Yes . . . yes . . . Good, you should get boycott! You should.'

Denise   She exclaimed with panted breath.

Jules   'I'm so tired of it all . . . I'm exhausted . . . depleted . . . with having to try and make these people understand, make she pay yes . . . good . . . brute.'

Denise   I got my phone out to check myself. Notification after notification after rhaated notification. Thank God I had set it on silent or it would have sounded like a symphony of hate.

Jules   'Look pon dis, dis ya white woman saying she's bored of woke . . . bored of woke. "We should get rid of wokeness?" Like it was hers to get rid of . . . "we" invented "woke"'

Denise   Jules said slapping her chest so hard she made it sound hollow.

Jules   'So "we" could cope and try to understand what is happening to us and then dem come teef it and now say "they" are bored of it . . . wouldn't dream of imagining how fucking bored, angry, frustrated, depressed, hurt, boxed in, unloved "we" feel having to "be" bloody woke?'

Denise   Out of nowhere her eyes became a waterfall, as unbounded emotion poured from her.

Jules 'Woven so tight with wokeness, so as not to walk into a school and shoot kids, white people, like they shoot us . . . jail us . . . patronise us . . . woke enough to deal with the likes of your Carly . . . "Just learn the lyrics" she said . . . cos she really thinks hip hop is just about music don't she? No matter what words are rapped, that it's just about selling a song . . . that it's just for entertainment . . . we are just entertainment . . . just a way to get some black cock. Boycott it yes . . . fuck it all.'

Then Cynthia tried to squeeze love back into Jules. Whilst staring at me as if I was wearing a MAGA hat and a UKIP t-shirt.

Cynthia 'Look, someone is saying what's offensive about it . . . can you believe dat . . . shows they must say worse on a regular innit . . . "Heard worse so what's the beef?" Well, we have too, innit? Which is why I agree to boycott your rass, Denise . . . cos this is just another thin layer of shit, on the thick shit sandwich we eat . . . daily . . . and I've just about had enough . . . yeah I'll sign that petition even if that means hurting you, Denise . . . fuck her and fuck you too.'

Silence.

Carly I said sorry to them. I said sorry from the bottom of my heart.

Denise What do you think you are? A subatomic superposition?

Carly Eh?

Denise A suba . . . look it up . . . see I did A level physics . . . which clearly you didn't.

Carly No /

Denise Which is why when you look at me like I'm an idiot, I look at you like this.

She gives 'the look'.

Carly   What you going on about?

Denise   Have you ever listened to your 'apology'?

Carly   . . .

Denise   Objectively?

Carly   No.

Denise   Let's do it /

Carly   No! /

Denise   Together . . . here . . . I'll find it /

Carly   No /

Denise   should be easy /

Carly   please /

Denise   Oh, look, bloody easy . . . there you are.

She presses play. We see her, feel her . . . somehow we experience this in an immersive way.

Carly   'Dear Offended, I sit here now knowing my . . . well . . . that our business is now ruined, over . . . dead. Some of you will see this a good thing considering. Obviously I don't . . . my mum and dad worked their arses off to pay the mortgage on our house, which when Dad died, Mum sold to give us the opportunity to buy this shop coupled with Delroy's mum's savings too. Obvs there's the hard work and pain and hopes that went into keeping my dad's florist running and Dee and Delroy's takeaway . . . so this is gutting for me cos erm . . . erm, I guess the fault . . .

'Blame, the erm, erm . . . cause is me . . . me . . . me and my drunken nonsense. I suppose nothing I can say will get me out of this . . . I'm now seen as a racist and this message won't go viral like my . . . my five . . . you know, erm . . . cos well, we aren't really after the truth no more are we? Who's gonna repost this? Right wing, left wing, far this, far fucking that, no one seems to want to own, except . . . we're just finding our way . . . ain't we? We just finding our . . . .

'You know I can't walk down my street . . . without some . . . one saying something but I bet Farage or Boris can walk down the street and none of you say a word? Dominic Cummings or Katie what's her name . . . you'd probably ask for a selfie just for a laugh . . . but me with a mixed-race . . . oh fuck better get that right . . . dual heritage . . . global majority . . . I mean what's the word YOU get ME to call MY! . . . DAUGHTER.

'. . . MY . . . DAUGHTER. My baby girl. Who will grow up one day and see all this hate for her mum online, question my love for her dad and hate me and hate herself . . . When you will have forgotten my name . . . as you saunter onto the next poor sod to get it wrong . . . The next poor cow you make a call to social fucking services about, next fucker you can ruin . . . cancel. Alright, alright, alright, truth is I did it. Yeah I did it too . . . gave some bastards a right good kicking online . . . yeah lots of angry face emojis at someone saying something disgraceful, doing something I disagreed with . . . something I thought . . . wrong. Oh yeah . . . right loved it me . . . tap, tap, tap, tap, tap. Up to twenty-odd red angry face emojis . . . Oh yeah . . . . . . yeah but let me tell you . . . when you fuck up, yeah you with ya virtue signalling, vegan fucking trainers on . . . or you with *Sunday Telegraph* magazine that "happens" to be on your kitchen sideboard. When you do, you'll see how fucking lonely it is when friends are too scared to be associated with ya . . . scared the stench of social media failure will affect how many likes they get for another phony, filtered, over the shoulder, look at my arse please Instagram post. When you find yourself persona non grata . . . considered a straight-up . . . cunt.

Cos it will . . . one day I promise one day you'll get your pronoun wrong . . . back the wrong influencer, like the wrong article, repost the wrong book, eat an advofuckingcado from a sanctioned country. Use the wrong make-up company, have wrong job to be able to dance at a party, suck the wrong knob.'

Tears stream from her face.

'You remember me . . . remember me asking, begging for forgiveness . . . begging for my life back . . . my life . . . cos you've taken my life, when you've lost your social standing as I have, remember you didn't give a shit about me and mine.'

She turns off the phone.

It didn't quite go as I planned

Denise   No shit.

Carly   I thought going live would be more –

Denise   Stupid?

Carly   Sincere . . . I least I can say that was me /

Denise   Well, it went viral . . . which was what you wanted.

Carly   Yeah /

Denise   But for the wrong reasons.

Carly   I am sorry though.

Denise   It don't cut it, Carly . . .

Carly   Eh? But I meant it /

Denise   Welcome to the world of black.

Carly   What?

Denise   You think cos you know a little about one black man you know all sorts of different black cultures . . . people?

Carly   I was drunk.

Denise   But honestly, welcome . . . welcome . . . cos one thing you'll understand now, which you clearly didn't get . . . with all you've been through with Michael and Delroy . . . your dad, mum . . . when you walk with blackness . . . You don't get nothing for free with anyone . . . including from blacks.

Carly   Oh here we go . . . you lot think you've got the monopoly on wisdom?

Denise   No but we have got a monopoly on always having to start from the beginning no matter what has gone before . . . I think that's why black people love the idea of fame so much . . . so they can walk in a room with the assumption people think that they are somebody, so they can walk in a room with dignity . . . their dignity . . . because most assumptions about us mean . . . like you now, that you come from shit . . . know shit or have done some shit that you should be ashamed of.

So you have to prove yourself in the corner shop, on the bus, in your workplace, on the job, in your car, on a bike, playing netball, eating food, everywhere and everything is like a way to prove your worth . . . and now you have to do the same . . . your gonna have to prove yourself, earn it every hour, every minute, every bloody day . . . so welcome to the world of black, Carly.

Carly   I hear you, Denise /

Denise   Good. I was offered a job.

Carly   Say?

Denise   As a chef.

Carly   Say!

Denise   Some posh West End place. This white guy who owns it came into the shop, he ate two patties. At first I thought he wanted to buy all of my patties outright, but it turned out at he wanted me to make my patties at his gaff. Don't look at me like that.

Carly (*pissed off*)   Wow!

Denise   Me as a chef, it was my dream, you have no idea.

(*Points to the audience.*) But this lot do.

(*To the audience.*) Innit?

Carly   All this chat that you're giving, and you're sorted with another job.

Denise   Hence the words 'was offered', Carly, it ain't happening. One minute it was all agreed, I was good to, all that was left was my rehearsed chat with my son. 'You got this, boy, you don't need me, blah, blah, blah.' Next was you, dropping the mike, all over social media. Followed quickly was an email. 'Dear Mrs Tomlin, we regret to inform you . . .' blah bloody blah.

Carly   You can't keep blaming me for everything, Denise. Remember. Me. You. Shop. Covid. Broke!

Denise   Have you not been listening, Carly, do you not get it? It's not about blame. It's not about whether that restaurant guy saw your performance, finds out we're related and puts two and two. Or even if he changed his mind or someone changed it for him. It's about black, girl, and how we are always feeling about baing black! It ain't about right, it ain't about wrong, it's about feel! You get?

Carly   I get. I get it, Denise.

Denise   Do you? For real, Carly?

Carly   Why the bloody hell isn't Delroy here with us, right now? Why aren't they both here?

Denise   Innit!

Carly   They should be here, the dozy pricking pricks.

Denise   Innit!

Carly   I don't give a flying if it's Leyton Orient, I don't give a fuck that they are beating Man U, they should be here.

Denise   They're not.

Carly   I know they are not, I can bloody well see they are not here.

Denise   They are not beating Man U.

Carly Man U score? So what's the damage?

Denise Two goals in two minutes. Man U are 2–1 up!

(*Listens to the radio.*) Final whistle.

Carly They must be crying.

Laughs.

Oh babe, what I wouldn't give to see the looks on both of their faces right now.

Denise Do you care?

Carly Like fuck! Worst day of our lives and they fuck off out of it to watch a ball being kicked about. I hate them. And I love them. The twats.

Denise (*agrees*) Right!

Carly How fucked is that?

Denise When the man arrives, we just hand the keys over and go . . . yeah?

Carly Yeah . . .

Denise It was fun while it lasted. But now it's over.

Carly You know if you want to cry a little, you can.

Denise Who said I'm crying?

Carly I'm not saying it. I'm just saying if you want to.

Denise Well, I'm not. What's done is done.

Carly I know I've wanted to.

Denise Good for you.

Carly I even had a quick weep inside when I went in to get this.

Shows the bottle.

Denise Congratulations.

Carly   I came close a few weeks back as well when I had to tell Mum on Facetime, tanning herself in Majorca she was, all over, no white bits.

Her sun-tan lotion must be factor fucking zero . . . She's gunna get skin cancer if she carries on like that. Anyhow's, I told her all about it, that we were going under, both shops, not bleeding well happy was an understatement. Going on about me and Michael have always let her down. She wished she never had us, that out of the three of us Lisa is her favourite, which I thought was a bit strong.

Her right I suppose, it was her life savings she handed over to us, so it's ok to let a few tears out, Denise, that is all I am saying to you.

Denise   Anytime you want to stop talking, Carly, it's allowed.

Carly   I don't mean those things I said at the hen do, Denise . . . I don't think you're foolish or jealous or think your culture is mine, Denise.

Denise   Yeah, well.

Carly   Hand on heart, God's honest, I think you are the most charismatic, courageous, audacious and deeply feminine woman I have ever met.

Denise   Are you trying to make me cry here? Are you, Carly? Cos it ain't gunna work.

Carly   I'm proud that you're my family. I am proud you're my mother in sin. I love you, Denise . . . and I really love your son . . . with everything I possess . . . I am so so sorry.

Denise   What is this? What is this about?

Carly   The truth.

Denise   The truth? I want you to tell me another truth?

Carly   Such as?

Denise   And you have to be straight with me about this?

Carly   What?

Beat.

Denise   Cos if yer lying, I will find the nearest sharpest thing there is to juke you with.

Carly   What's your question, Denise?

Denise   Can you really do a low fade on Delroy's hair?

Carly (*boasts*)   Like a pro.

Denise *laughs.*

Denise   I've heard it all now.

Carly   Don't look now, Denise, but you're laughing.

Denise   I suppose I am.

Carly   I love him so much, you know. I swear to you.

Denise   You can't love my boy that much without knowing him. You'll both work it out, somehow.

Carly   I want to cut all of his bloody trainers into a thousand pieces though. Every last one. Dozens of them, Denise, fucking hundreds.

Taking up space in our bedroom, like they are a virus. Does that make me a bad person?

Denise   Babe, I'll lend you the knife.

Carly   Does that still make me a Fletcher?

Denise   What do you think?

Carly   I'm not like them. I'm a Fletcher, Denise, but I am not Dad's Fletcher. Or Michael's. I'm not, Dee!

Denise (*sincere*)   I know it, Carly. I know it.

They see a car pulling up.

Oh God . . . That him? Is that the buyer?

Carly   Parking?

Denise   Yeah.

Carly   Yeah . . . it is.

Denise   . . .

Carly   Denise? You alright?

Denise   I'm gonna cry . . . shit . . . I'm gonna cry.

Carly   Oh, babe, come here!

They hug. It becomes a warm embrace. They hold each other tightly. They both cry.

Denise   This don't mean I completely forgive you, you know.

Carly   I know.

She wipes **Denise***'s tear.*

Carly   I got you, yeah. You got me.

Denise *nods.*

Carly *looks up at the shop one last time.*

A fucking GAIL's! After everything . . .

Denise   It's closing time, Carly. It's over. Come on, babe, let's do this.

Carly *takes* **Denise***'s hand. We hear footsteps.*

The two women turn to face the man. **Denise** *holds out the front-door keys.*

Blackout.